ian Animals

Emus

Big
Buddy **BOOKS**
Australian Animals

ABDO
Publishing Company

by **Julie Murray**

VISIT US AT
www.abdopublishing.com

Published by ABDO Publishing Company, 8000 West 78th Street, Edina, Minnesota 55439.

Copyright © 2012 by Abdo Consulting Group, Inc. International copyrights reserved in all countries. No part of this book may be reproduced in any form without written permission from the publisher. Big Buddy Books™ is a trademark and logo of ABDO Publishing Company.

Printed in the United States of America, North Mankato, Minnesota.
052011
092011

 PRINTED ON RECYCLED PAPER

Coordinating Series Editor: Rochelle Baltzer
Editor: Marcia Zappa
Contributing Editors: Megan M. Gunderson, BreAnn Rumsch, Sarah Tieck
Graphic Design: Maria Hosley
Cover Photograph: *Getty Images*: Tier Und Naturfotografie J & C Sohns.
Interior Photographs/Illustrations: *Getty Images*: Fred Bavendam/Minden Pictures (p. 25), Christopher Groenhout (p. 17), Stefan Posties (p. 8), David Trood (p. 11); *iStockphoto*: ©iStockphoto.com/Byronsdad (pp. 5, 21), ©iStockphoto.com/candyfloss (p. 13), ©iStockphoto.com/clearviewstock (p. 27), ©iStockphoto.com/CraigRJD (p. 7), ©iStockphoto.com/garyforsyth (p. 12), ©iStockphoto.com/idizimage (p. 19), ©iStockphoto.com/JohnCarnemolla (pp. 19, 29), ©iStockphoto.com/Matejay (p. 4), ©iStockphoto.com/ozflash (p. 23), ©iStockphoto.com/photosbyash (p. 9), ©iStockphoto.com/RachelKathrynGiles (p. 27), ©iStockphoto.com/Redzaal (p. 9), ©iStockphoto.com/robynmac (p. 9), ©iStockphoto.com/RollingEarth (p. 24), ©iStockphoto.com/seraphic06 (p. 8), ©iStockphoto.com/TimothyBall (p. 4); *Photo Researchers, Inc.*: ANT Photo Library (p. 23), *Photolibrary*: Peter Arnold Images (p. 15); *Shutterstock*: Eleanor (p. 17), Image Focus (p. 11).

Library of Congress Cataloging-in-Publication Data

Murray, Julie, 1969-
  Emus / Julie Murray.
    p. cm. -- (Australian animals)
  ISBN 978-1-61783-010-5
  1. Emus--Juvenile literature. I. Title.
  QL696.C34M87 2012
  598.5'24--dc22
                              2011002297

Contents

Amazing Australian Animals 4

Emu Territory 6

Welcome to the Continent Down Under! 8

Take a Closer Look 10

Grounded 14

Mealtime 18

On the Move 20

Family Life 22

Incredible Eggs 24

Baby Emus 26

Survivors 28

Crikey! I'll bet you never knew... 30

Important Words 31

Web Sites 31

Index 32

Long ago, nearly all land on Earth was one big mass. About 200 million years ago, the land began to break into **continents**. One of these is an island called Australia.

Emus are known for their size and speed.

Australia is home to many interesting animals. One of these animals is the emu. Emus are large birds that cannot fly. Wild emus are found only in Australia. Emus are also raised on farms around the world.

Emu Territory

Emus live almost everywhere in Australia. They are commonly found on grassy plains and in open forests. But, they can also live on coasts and in mountains. The only places emus don't normally live are deserts, rain forests, and cities.

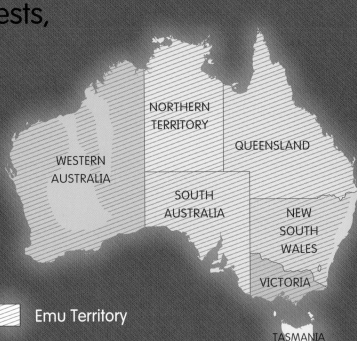

NORTHERN TERRITORY

QUEENSLAND

WESTERN AUSTRALIA

SOUTH AUSTRALIA

NEW SOUTH WALES

VICTORIA

TASMANIA

 Emu Territory

Emus used to live on several islands near Australia. But, these populations died out long ago. Now, wild emus are only found on the main continent.

Welcome to the Continent Down Under!

If you took a trip to where emus live, you might find…

…a prime minister.

The prime minister is the head of Australia's government. In 2010, Julia Gillard became the first female prime minister of Australia. The national coat of arms stands for Australia's government. It has an emu on it!

...the outback.

The center of Australia is called the outback. This large area has harsh land and weather. So, very few people live there. Much of it is open country and feeding grounds for farm animals, including emus. Wild emus live in parts of the outback, too.

...acacia plants.

Acacia bushes and trees are some of Australia's most common plants. The continent has almost 1,000 different types of acacias. Australians call them wattles. They are common in the open forests emus live in.

Take a Closer Look

Emus are the tallest birds native to Australia. They grow to be five to six feet (1.5 to 1.8 m) tall. They weigh up to 120 pounds (54 kg). Female emus are bigger than males.

Uncovered!

Emus are part of a family of large, flightless birds called ratites. Other ratites include ostriches, kiwis, rheas, and cassowaries. In the wild, these animals are only found on Earth's southern half.

9 ft (2.7 m)

6 ft (1.8 m)

3 ft (0.9 m)

man   emu   ostrich

Emus (*left*) are the second-tallest birds in the world. Only ostriches (*above*) are taller.

An emu has a short, round body. So how does it get so tall? It has two long legs and a long neck! An emu also has big feet. And, it has a small head with a pointed beak.

An emu's neck and head are partly bare with bluish skin. Its body has thick feathers that are gray, brown, or black. Unlike many birds, most of an emu's feathers aren't stiff. They are soft and often look like shaggy hair.

Uncovered!
Emus have stiff tail feathers. Sometimes, they rattle their tails to try to scare predators.

An emu's soft feathers don't keep it as dry as stiff feathers would. But, they help keep an emu cool in the hot Australian sun.

Grounded

Emus have wings. But, these birds are not built to fly. Their wings are only about seven inches (18 cm) long! That is shorter than a crow's wings. And, their wings lack stiff feathers to help lift them into the air.

Uncovered!
Emus are strong swimmers.

An emu's wings are so short they are often hidden by feathers.

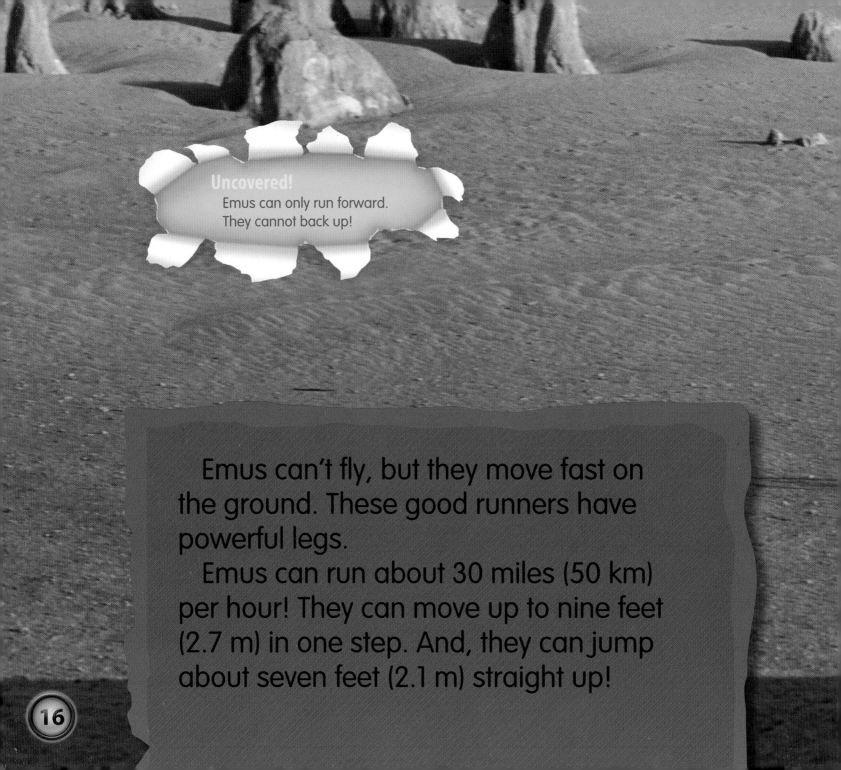

Uncovered!

Emus can only run forward.
They cannot back up!

Emus can't fly, but they move fast on the ground. These good runners have powerful legs.

Emus can run about 30 miles (50 km) per hour! They can move up to nine feet (2.7 m) in one step. And, they can jump about seven feet (2.1 m) straight up!

Emus use their great speed to escape most predators. These include wild dogs called dingoes (*right*). Emus can also kick predators with their big feet!

Mealtime

Emus spend their days searching for food. They use their beaks to eat many different plants and small animals. These include seeds, grass, flowers, fruit, insects, and lizards.

Uncovered!
Sometimes, emus eat the poop of other animals!

Emus need a lot of water. They drink two to five gallons (8 to 19 L) each day.

Emus eat whatever food is available. For example, they may eat seeds during dry times. After a rainfall, they may eat fresh grass.

On the Move

Emus generally live alone. But, they sometimes form large flocks where food is plentiful.

Emus stay in one area as long as they have enough food and water. But if they run out of these, emus **migrate**. Sometimes, they travel more than ten miles (16 km) a day.

Uncovered!

When food is plentiful, emus store fat in their bodies. This fat keeps them alive when food becomes hard to find. As they use up stored fat, adult emus can lose more than half of their weight!

In Western Australia, emu flocks tend to migrate with the seasons. They move north in the summer and south in the winter.

Family Life

Each year, adult male and female emus form pairs for **mating**. The male emu makes a nest on the ground out of twigs, leaves, and grass. Then, the female emu lays 5 to 15 eggs in the nest. She lays one egg every few days.

After all the eggs are laid, the female emu leaves. The male emu sits on the nest to warm the eggs. He stays there for about eight weeks.

Uncovered!
Female emus may mate with more than one male each year. They can lay up to three groups of eggs yearly.

Emu nests are generally round. They measure about two to four feet (0.6 to 1.2 m) across.

While a father emu sits on a nest, he doesn't eat, drink, pee, or poop. He only stands to turn the eggs or pull in an egg that has rolled out.

Incredible Eggs

Emu eggs are usually dark green. They have thick shells with bumpy surfaces. An emu egg is large. It can weigh more than one pound (0.5 kg)! And, it can be as long as five inches (13 cm).

One emu egg is about as heavy as 12 chicken eggs!

An emu egg's thick shell helps keep the chick inside safe.

Baby Emus

Emu chicks **hatch** after about eight weeks. At birth, they are around ten inches (25 cm) tall.

At first, emu chicks stay in the nest while their father feeds them. After three to ten days, the chicks can feed themselves. Then, they leave the nest. Emu chicks stay with their father for about a year and a half.

When they first hatch, emu chicks are tan with brown stripes. Their feathers change color as they grow.

Emu fathers show their chicks how to find food and stay safe.

Survivors

Over the years, emus have faced many dangers. Long ago, farmers killed them for eating crops and destroying fences. Today, dingoes hunt them for food. And, **droughts** make food and water hard to find.

Still, emus **survive**. Today, about 600,000 to 700,000 wild emus live in Australia. And, emus are popular farm animals around the world. These special animals help make Australia an amazing place.

In the wild, emus can live 10 to 20 years.

Uncovered!
Farmers raise emus for their meat, leather, and oil. Emu oil is used in lotions, soaps, shampoos, and other products.

Crikey!
I'll bet you never knew...

...that emus are loud! Emus make several noises including hissing, grunting, and booming. An emu's boom sounds like a low drum. It can be heard about one mile (2 km) away!

...that emus help grow plants. Emus eat seeds and then walk to new places. When they poop, the seeds come out and sometimes grow into new plants!

...that the sun was created when a large emu egg was tossed into the sky and exploded into fire. Not really! But an ancient Australian story explains it this way.

Important Words

continent one of Earth's seven main land areas.

drought (DRAUT) a long period of dry weather.

hatch to be born from an egg.

mate to join as a couple in order to reproduce, or have babies.

migrate to move from one place to another to find food or have babies.

survive to continue to live or exist.

Web Sites

To learn more about emus, visit ABDO Publishing Company online. Web sites about emus are featured on our Book Links page. These links are routinely monitored and updated to provide the most current information available.

www.abdopublishing.com

Index

acacia plants **9**

Australia **4, 5, 6, 7, 8, 9, 10, 13, 21, 28, 30**

body **12, 14, 15, 16, 17, 18, 20**

chicks **25, 26, 27**

dangers **13, 17, 28**

dingoes **17, 28**

eating habits **18, 19, 20, 23, 26, 27, 30**

eggs **22, 23, 24, 25, 30**

farms **5, 9, 28, 29**

feathers **12, 13, 14, 15, 27**

flocks **20, 21**

Gillard, Julia **8**

habitat **6, 7, 9**

mating **22**

migrating **20, 21**

nests **22, 23, 26**

ostriches **10, 11**

outback **9**

ratites **10**

running **5, 16, 17**

size **5, 10, 11, 12, 26**